My HEART Leaks Ink

Poetic Expressions for Restoration and Empowerment

Written By:
Brooksie B. Sturdivant, Ed.D.

Copyright© 2021 by Dr. Brooksie Sturdivant

Published by Johnson Tribe Publishing, LLC Atlanta, GA

All rights reserved, including the express right to reproduce this book or portions thereof in any form whatsoever whether now known or hereinafter developed. For information address Johnson Tribe Publishing, P.O. Box 1587 Powder Springs, Georgia 30127.

This book may not be copied or reproduced without the express written permission of the author or publisher. The author is also available for speaking engagements and may be contacted by visiting www.3ellc.org.

Manufactured in the United States of America

ISBN- 978-1-7363274-8-7

FIRST EDITION

Illustration: Courtney Monday

USA: $14.99

Dedication

This book is dedicated to those experiencing
what seems like a combination of
hell and high water.
I beseech you to choose the *narrow way,*
so you can truly become *free indeed.*

Introduction

I was born in the late 1970s into what might seem like a "normal" family. My family included a father, a mother, and a brother who was born seven years before I was. We lived together in a small, brick, three-bedroom house in a small, rural town. Both of my parents were employed, and we owned an automobile. We even had a pet German Shepherd dog. Nevertheless, when I was two years old, things took a turn when my mother was diagnosed with schizophrenia, a mental disorder that causes hallucinations and paranoia. Some family members and adults in our town said it was because of me. They said that age 37, seven years after she had my brother, was "too old to be having a baby" and that maybe postpartum depression drove her crazy. There is no reason a child should have ever heard these different viewpoints, but I heard them, and I believed them. My father could not take it – the schizophrenia – and the changes in my mom's behavior, so he left. I do not recall him living with us. He left when I was around three years old. From that point, we lived with my maternal grandmother, but that was brief; she passed away a year and a half later when I was about to turn six years old.

In the years to come, I longed to experience normalcy. Nothing about my childhood was normal; yet, it is the norm for many children who experience household dysfunction. I noticed signs of physical and emotional neglect as early as age six after my maternal grandmother passed away. By age eight, I concluded and internally professed, "No one is in charge of me!" Despite the unstable circumstances, I was determined to rise above my predicament and ensure my adulthood was better than my childhood. Schooling was a place of agency and resilience, and I believed from an early age that education was the key to my very existence. Consequently, I was academically resilient and excelled in grade school and undergraduate college.

Nevertheless, the social and emotional effects from the neglect and extreme pressure to perform were overwhelming. I was oftentimes fearful, anxious, and full of shame. Considering my introverted tendencies, I internalized those negative emotions. This internalization affected my self-perception, esteem, and confidence, and thus my interpersonal relationships. I struggled in silence while screaming on the inside. I do not claim to be an exceptional poet, but from a place of pain, I learned to embrace the power of the pen. As early as fourth grade, I fell in love with words and their usefulness for self-expression, and during my adolescent and young adult years, writing became a means of coping amidst the chaos. I turned to journaling and poetry writing to confess my concerns and to face my frustrations and fears. I allowed *my heart to leak ink*. Therefore, some of the poems in this anthology reflect raw emotion and hints of immaturity. "Judge not, lest ye be judged." I allow you in with hopes that you'll find a way out.

About this Book

My Heart Leaks Ink: Poetic Reflections for Restoration and Empowerment includes 47 poems I wrote from 1992 to 2015 between ages 13 and 37. As a compilation, the poems reflect the process of my evolution from girlhood to womanhood amidst adversity. The book is divided into three parts, reflecting three phases, which I believe are key to personal restoration and empowerment. The parts progress from the pains of my *Past* to an analysis of the then *Present*, which is necessary to manifest hope for a brighter *Future* and the courage to embrace all you are to be. The three parts are titled as follows:

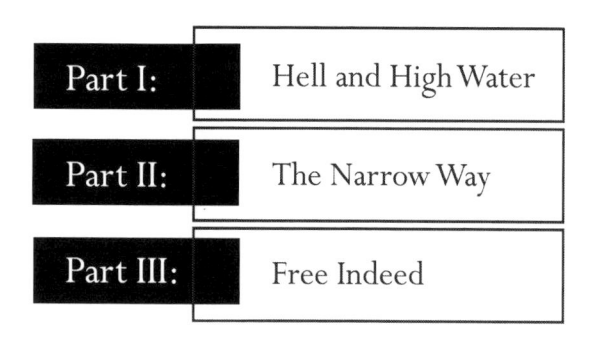

Part I:	Hell and High Water
Part II:	The Narrow Way
Part III:	Free Indeed

I share this collection of poems to:

- Highlight the long-term social and emotional effects of adverse childhood experiences.
- Inspire women, especially young girls, to persevere. Brighter days can and will come if you take action and believe. Know that it is a process; learn and grow along the way. Times may get tough, but you will endure.
- Provoke parents and practitioners (teachers, social workers, counselors, community agencies) to intervene. Resilience can manifest with the proper social and emotional supports. We, adults, must be the change we wish to see.

When necessary, I provide background information to add context to select poems. I also include the date I composed each poem, which can reveal my age at the time based on my birth date, August 26, 1978.

Although I use Bible scriptures to emphasize some of my thoughts and feelings, I do not profess to be a preacher or trained minister. However, I believe I am an epistle of Christ (2 Corinthians 3:3), and I share to simply let my light shine to glorify God (Matthew 5:16 NKJV).

As you read, I encourage you to *CONNECT* to the content of each poem, *REFLECT* on how it speaks to your past or present circumstances, *CORRECT* that which is holding you back, *PROJECT* optimism towards a fulfilled future.

You can overcome! I believe in you!

Table of Contents

Dedication	3
Introduction	4
About this Book	6
Table of Contents	8

Part I: Hell and High Water — 11

A. *Friend or Foe* — 13

All About Me	15
Respect	16
Woman to Woman	17
Nobody Bothers Me	18

B. *Looking for Love* — 19

When I Loved You	21
Love Me Today	22
Gone Away	23
Breaking My Heart	24
When You're with Me	25
Confrontation	26

C. *Cold, Cold World*	27
Why?	29
Thick and Thin	30
Hide Away	31
Trapped	32
Naughty Potty	33
Heaviness	34
Part II: The Narrow Way	35
A. *This or That*	37
What is Rain?	39
Lyrics	40
Plight of a Pusher	41
Somebody Told You a Lie	42
Reading Really is Fundamental	43
B. *Better Than Bitter*	44
My Apology	46
Physical	47
Apart	48
Who?	49
Emotions	50
Contraceptive	51
C. *Write the Vision*	52
If	54
I'll be Leaving Soon	55

Abandoned Ship	56
Through God's Eyes	57

Part III: Free Indeed — 58

A. *Yet Will*	60
God the Father	62
The Prayer I Pray for You	63
King Solomon's Temple	64
Pathway to an Upgrade	65
Process for Progress	66
You've Been Drafted	67
B. *Far Above Rubies*	68
Unfulfilled	70
Thank You	71
Falling	72
Normalcy	73
Desire	74
C. *Survive to Thrive*	75
Make It Happen	77
Manners Matter	78
Bold and Beautiful Brooksie	79
Questions, Comments, or Concerns?	80
Fly, Fly Away	81
About the Author	82

Part I: Hell and High Water

Darius Brooks wrote an old gospel hymn called "Fire Next Time" in reference to the Biblical story of Noah (Genesis 6:9 through Genesis 9:29; 2 Peter 3: 5-7). The lyrics present a warning that says, *"It's gonna rain; it's gonna rain! You better get ready, and bear this in mind. God showed Noah by the rainbow sign. No more water but fire next time!"* My adolescent years seemed like a constant combination of each, *Hell and High Water!* I recall times when I felt like I was drowning. There were also times when I burned with frustration and rage due to my circumstances. The 16 poems included in *Part I: Hell and High Water* consist mostly of those I wrote during tough times as a teenager.

Prior to my teen years, I recall being sweet and passive. As a preteen, I felt good about myself despite my situation, which I express in the first poem, "All About Me". I attempted to suppress my sadness through my skills, talents, and hobbies. Nevertheless, deep down, I was disappointed and afraid. I wanted someone, anyone, to recognize the anxiety I experienced due to the lack of maternal support I desired and needed. I still believed someone would come to my rescue. As I entered my teen years, that hope began to fade. I found myself looking for love in all the wrong places. Doubt set in followed by anger, envy, and pessimism. These negative emotions are expressed in these poems of which I am not proud. Part I is organized in three sections:

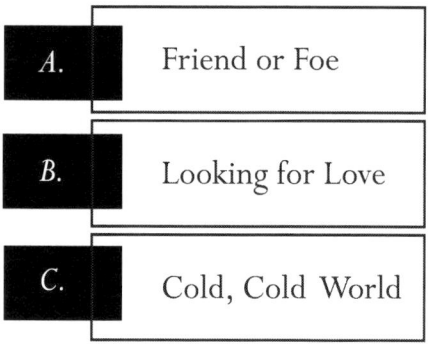

A. Friend or Foe

B. Looking for Love

C. Cold, Cold World

A. *Friend or Foe*

Friendship represents a significant aspect of adolescence. Fortunately, I grew up in a small, rural community where everybody knew everyone for the most part. The town was segregated by class and race. My neighborhood was literally on the "other side of the tracks" as a railroad track divided downtown from the low-income, residential area designated for African-American families. Despite minor competitions over hair texture, colorism, and body shape, I seemed to get along well with the girls in my neighborhood, partly because many of them were my distant cousins or related to a relative by marriage. Considering my light complexion, thin, curly hair, and narrow frame, I had to ensure my comebacks were strong. Needless to say, I developed a mean side-eye and learned to roll my eyes and curse like a sailor at an early age. It was all fun and games because between the cursing, we would double-dutch, build club houses, choreograph dance routines, and play yard games, like hide-and-seek. We expressed our creativity as a means to escape as each of us experienced varying household challenges. We supported one another then as we continue to do to this day.

Where there are friends, you will find foes. Despite my efforts, I learned early on, not everyone is going to like you. Many will search for reasons to not like you for no good reason. I have to admit, the rejection can hurt. I processed others' disdain for me personally, believing it was due to something I lacked. For a long time, I related whatever I supposedly lacked directly to my lack of mothering, which added to my frustration. This cycle became a self-fufilling prophesy: I wanted people to like me. They didn't for whatever reason. As a result, I became more insecure and got an attitude, which caused people to dislike me all the more and so on and so on. The five poems in this section show how I transformed from a confident and carefree preteen to a frustrated and critical high schooler as I reflect on the lack of loyalty and the decline in dignity among *Friends and Foes.*

All About Me

Written March 1992

I am a girl who loves to go to school.
I love school because I think it's cool.
I love to dance and roller skate,
but doing science is what I hate.

I have long hair and brown eyes.
When it comes to math, I seem to be wise.
When I go home, I bring books along.
When I get there, I talk on the phone.

I go to church and in the choir I sing.
I like to write, draw, and all those things.
These are some things I thought you should know.
Sorry to tell you, but I've gotta go!

Respect

Written June 5, 1995

Respect is a thing that I wanted to have,
but now I see that I never will.
The people that I respect and care for,
never respect the way I feel.

Respect is something you gain for yourself,
then you can respect another.
Most people have no respect for themselves,
so how can they respect their brother?

I try to show respect,
so I'll receive respect in return.
Yet, I'm the only one who respects me.
Respect yourself, that's all I've learned!

People have no respect for their bodies.
It's sad because now I see.
If you can't respect yourself,
How can you respect me?

Woman to Woman

Written October 31, 1995

Woman describes me; I never quit, I try.
Experienced many heartaches, but no one hears my cry.
Beaten and battered but on my soul will go.
Keeping my faith as my wisdom seems to grow.

Only been broken by my choices in men.
I respect my mind and body, so I'll never hurt again.
I'll never choose another if there's pain I foresee.
I'd rather be alone than unhappy.

Men with women, I show your girls much respect.
Sharing a man with a woman, I know I will regret.
Save your games and lies if your love is untrue.
Life's too short for me to play, so without you I'll have to do.

Are you a real woman? Do you respect your body and heart?
Will you respect me with my man, or will you tear my world apart?
There are two different types of women: Real and Fake.
Give in order to receive, but all you know is take.

No, you're not a real woman; you're just a little girl.
You disrespect yourself and slowly wreck my world.
If you don't respect yourself then nobody can.
Take my advice, little girl, be a real woman.

Nobody Bothers Me

Written February 3, 1996

At the death of me, you would rejoice.
I hear your comments and your angry voice.
You'd laugh if you saw me hanging from a tree.
I'd be gasping for air, but you wouldn't help me.
If I fell in the street and broke my leg,
I'd cry and plea; for your help, I'd beg.
You'd walk on by, laugh, and tell your friends.
Smile in my face and then talk behind my back again.
Pointing and whispering when I pass by.
Spread your rumors and tell your lies.
You hate my guts to the highest degree,
but still, nobody bothers me.

B. Looking for Love

    Acquiring a first kiss, high school sweetheart, and prom date proved difficult. With small-town living comes countless cousins, which translates to few dating options. Considering my slim, curveless frame and frizzy, untamable hair, the quest seemed all the more challenging. I encountered my first kiss at age 13, which proved to be wet and gross. I was also 13-years-old when I experienced my first menstrual cycle, which we called *"my period"*. By then, I had realized informing my mother or asking her for guidance was pointless. I relied on tips from a copy of *Are You There, God? It's Me, Margaret!* that I had swiped from my third-grade classroom library, and I recall my neighborhood friends, whom I referred to as homegirls, teaching me what to do to manage my hygiene that week.

    With the hormonal changes came an increased desire for affection. While most of my peers pursued sex and physical attractions, I preferred an emotional connection. Even though I fell prey to the physical desires, I longed for a deep relationship with someone. I sought what I lacked – stability and consistency. I wanted to be loved. Reflecting, my expectations for what a boy could and would offer were unrealistic. Nevertheless, that did not prevent me from *Looking for Love* in all the wrong places.

The six poems in this section reveal my deep desire for love and the disappointment and frustration I experienced at every failed attempt to give and receive the love I longed for.

When I Loved You

Written June 26, 1995

I see you've got a new love, so why you wanna swing my way?
At least that's what you said when we talked the other day.
I know I said I'd always love you, and I said you were as sweet as wine.
But I didn't want your girlfriend's man; I wanted you to be mine.

I never wanted to share you, but I see the whole time I did.
I thought you were a man, but I see you're only a kid.
What's wrong with your new girl? She's pretty and loves you a lot.
She's giving you sex, but you call me, when you're alone and suddenly get hot.

I keep my pride and sadly say, "No. Why don't you call your girl?"
She'll never know how considerate I am; I'd never want to wreck her world.
I don't want to be like the girl who violated when you were mine.
By the way, where were you when I wanted to spend some time?

When I needed a kiss and hug, with no remorse, you gave them away.
All I wanted was the truth, but a lie was all you could say.
My love was always there for you; you walked out on me.
I wasn't going anywhere, but you were too blind to see.

You were never honest with me. In you, I had no trust.
You laughed, you left, you did not care, when my poor, little heart you crushed.
I expressed my feelings to you; there was nothing I'd ever hide.
You took advantage of my love and stripped me of my pride.

I needed more than sex; you really thought that was all?
Well, the next time the heat is on, give your new girlfriend a call.
Love comes in a package: honesty, trust, and understanding.
You paid no attention to my feelings. Your guilt made you demanding.

You act as if nothing happened after you lied and left me blue.
Can you even remember where you were, those days when I loved you?

Love Me Today

October 9, 1995

Yesterday, I gave you a call because you were on my mind.
You said you had to go for someone else was on the line.

Today, I asked you for a favor, but you had something to do.
I needed to see your smile and feel your touch, but your priority is you.

Tomorrow, I'll ask you the same; even though, you won't have time for me.
I'll need to talk about things on my mind, but you'll be too blind to see.

One day I know you'll decide to call, but there will be nothing I can do.
When I needed you, you did not care, so why should I attend to you?

It was you that I needed, your touch and your smile, but you chose to play.
Yesterday is gone, tomorrow is coming, why don't you just love me today?

Gone Away

Written November 27, 1995

You came in like the wind
on a cold winter day.
You brought me joy and happiness.
You showed me a better way.
You took away my troubles
and erased my inner pain.
You healed my broken heart
and took away the rain.
Now the seasons are changing;
summer's coming around.
The snow is gently fading,
Grass is growing on the ground.
You came in like the wind
 on a cold winter day.
Now all I have are memories.
My winter wind is gone away.

Breaking My Heart

Written January 23, 1996

BROKEN like a crystal glass,
shattered to the floor.

RIPPED like the rusted screen
of an old storm door.

CRUSHED like a juicy grape
after it is smashed and made to wine.

CORRUPTED like the brain
of a drug-infested mind.

TRAMPLED like a welcome mat
when guests enter your home.

HURT like the weeping widow
after death calls on her spouse.

ALONE like a baby chick
when its mother goes out for feed.

CRYING like a newborn babe,
for milk it's in desperate need.

SPLIT like a sheet of paper
after it's torn apart.

Can't you see, you're continuously, slowly breaking my heart?

When You're with Me

Written February 3, 1996

You rub my hair and kiss my lips,
massage my back and hug my hips.
Hold me tight and never let go.
When you're with me, it's true love you show.
You call me up and talk for hours.
I love our long walks and late-night showers.
You take me out and show me great things.
The thought of you, what joy it brings.
You share with me your secrets and dreams.
Together forever is the way it seems.
When I'm with you, all of these things occur.
But I don't even exist when you're with her.

Confrontation

Written October 13, 2004

Voices venting inside my head,

Outward expression, silence instead.

Lava imploding about to spew.

Confront or conceal, what should I do?

Aggravation rumbles, stirring animosity.

Navigate to decrease the velocity,

Overflowing as the tension grows.

I'm about to EXPLODE!

C. *Cold, Cold World*

    The lack of parental support and instability caused me to view the world as a dark, unsafe place. Coupled with my failures with foes and fake love affairs, I developed a pessimistic perspective of society as a whole. During these years, I was transient, moving from house to house with relatives and friends each time my mother was hospitalized for her condition. Despite their attempts to help with the situation, my needs exceeded their capacity to give, as no one can love and support you like a mother. Consequently, I began to view people as selfish and inconsiderate, even family members. During this time, I became more introverted and cerebral in my efforts to analyze, process, and cope with my everchanging surroundings and interactions.

    I began demonstrating concerns for humanity through my writing as early as age 14 in the first poem in this section titled "Why?". Pessimism, which I prefer to call realism, is a theme that persists throughout my poems as I am torn between what I desire and believe and what I observe and encounter consistently. Despite my faith in God, I can still say, I struggle with trusting mankind. Even now, humans never cease to amaze me. I wish I didn't care. I include six poems in this section to demonstrate my disdain and anxiety about that which I observed and experienced in this *Cold, Cold World*.

Why?

Written March 1992

"Why?" is a question we ask every day.
When you get hurt, why do you cry?
Why do you laugh, and why do you play?
When you are tired, why do you sigh?

Why is the world so bad?
Why are some people good?
Why do people always feel sad?
Why do we ask why? Do you think we should?

Why do we kill and shoot?
Why do we fuss and fight?
Why do we buy an expensive suit?
Why can't everything be alright?

"Why?" is a question we ask every day.
Why don't we just forget why and be on our way?

Thick and Thin

Written April 6, 1995

They say blood is thicker than water,
like the tear when I cry,
tears from my blood's wound to my back.
I cry, and I wonder, "Why?"

They say blood is thicker than water;
your blood stands by your side.
Yet, when needed most, they are gone,
because of their selfish pride.

I think my blood has run dry,
after all the pain.
They say blood is thicker than water.
I say, "It's as thin as rain!"

Hide Away

Written May 29, 1996

From the rain and the storms
The dark and gloomy day
From the ocean and the sea
I want to hide away
From the desert droughts
The tornadoes sweeping my way
From the snow and the hail
I want to hide away
From the crooked cops
And the children who disobey
From the sinful churches
I want to hide away
From the lonely nights
To the waking of the day
From this aching heart
I want to hide away
From the demon in me
Dear God I pray
From the demon in you
I want to hide away

Trapped

Written June 2, 1996

Throughout the years, I've figured it out,
this world is a trap that I'm caught in.
A world full of HATE—NO LOVE.
These demons are filled with sin.
Sex, drug, and violence, these are the three main things.
I almost forgot diseases like AIDS
spread from whores and one-night flings.
Am I the only one who notices
how this world is falling apart?
When it seems like my problems are over,
that's when they all seem to start.
They say if your heart stops beating,
the doctors consider you dead.
My heart is broken by the world and the beating has ceased;
instead of living, God, please call me home instead.
People wonder why I never smile
but clinch my fist and shout.
I'm trapped in a world full of HATE—NO LOVE,
and death is the only way out.

Naughty Potty

Written July 13, 2005

This poem reflects my experience as a 13-year-old eighth grader. The scenario occurred in Kernersville, NC in 1991. My friend and her little sister were trying to use the restroom at a store-front restaurant while her mother was in the grocery store. However, the clerk would not let us use the restroom due to our race.

What do you see when you look at me?
We were just children who simply had to pee!
Ding, dong, ding went the chime on the door.
He gazed with anger as if his eyes were sore.

He said, "What do you want?" as he blocked the doorway.
"To use the restroom," was all we could say.
"I don't know what Martin Luther King intended for you,
but if you think you're using this restroom, you must be a fool!"

We turned and ran as fast as we could!
What happened to loving your neighbor and simply being good?
Doesn't he see that my hair is long and my skin is light?
And if he'd research, he'd learn that my great-grandpa was white!

What about my pretty smile, Cherokee cheeks, and good grades?
I guess none of that matters when you're a black spade!
His words kept ringing, echoing in my head.
The more I recollected, the more I wanted him dead!

But what could I do since he was so cruel?
That day I learned that whiteness rules!
What do you see when you look at me?
We were just children who simply had to pee!

Heaviness

Written August 30, 2010

I have experienced…

broken friendships,
breakups,
death of loved ones,
car wrecks,
surgery,
rejection,
judgment,
slander,
misunderstanding,
betrayal…

…yet, I have known no pain that exceeds that which is evoked by the lack of a mother's love.

How can emptiness be so heavy?

Part II: The Narrow Way

In the Sermon on the Mount (Matthew Chapters 5-7), Jesus spoke to a large crowd and provided a number of dos and don'ts to obtain favor and be blessed, starting with The Beatitudes. Despite our free will as humans, He presented numerous imperative commands without a lot of options. However, in Chapter 7, verses 13 and 14, Jesus describes two gates as a metaphor for two paths from which we can choose as we navigate life. Jesus said,

13 "Enter by the narrow gate; for wide is the gate and broad is the way that leads to destruction, and there are many who go in by it. 14 Because narrow is the gate and difficult is the way which leads to life, and there are few who find it" (Matthew 7: 13-14 NKJV).

I remember making a mental note as a preteen to beware of the broad path.

Growing up in a rural town, I encountered quite a few paths during walks through the woods with cousins and friends. Broad paths were the easy ones. They were wide enough for two or three of us to walk side-by-side. There was less worry about spiders and webs, amphibians, rodents, and reptiles because you could see further down the path before you and along the edges. At times, there was enough space on each side for you to easily maneuver to avoid poison ivy plants and thorns, which we called *sticker briers*. Most times, you can see the destination well in advance, which can make it seem you are well on your way.

Nevertheless, I soon learned, just because it's easy, doesn't make it right. The narrow way can be lonely, there is no walking side-by-side. Someone must take the lead. You may get scratched and scraped because there is no space on the sides, and you are almost certain to walk through a spider web or two. The destination will be nowhere in sight. Due to fear, few will follow. Nevertheless, I found the narrow paths most rewarding. Just when the treks seemed to be a waste of time, we'd find abandoned houses to explore, relaxing ponds, or beautiful fields of flowers… treasures unknown. We would be amazed when the path took us to a familiar road, revealing a short cut.

The 15 poems in *Part II: The Narrow Way* reflect my struggle to decide. Considering my challenges with relationships and my pessimistic perspective, choosing *The Narrow Way* wasn't always easy. I wanted to fit in, be a part, and belong. Yet, despite free will, I knew I had to choose. Part II is organized in three sections:

A.	This or That
B.	Better Than Bitter
C.	Write the Vision

A. *This or That*

    The absence of parental guidance increased my struggle to navigate life during my teenage and young adult years. Like today, there were a lot of negative influences from peers, music, and media. Hip hop lyrics had begun to shift from the empowering, social justice messages of the 1980s to degrading women and condoning drug dealing in the 1990s. Education had become less of a priority. I recall analyzing every decision in detail and considering the pros and cons thoroughly, comparing what I heard to what I believed to be right. I often wondered, if I had a baby or got into trouble involving the police, who would help me? Furthermore, I was determined to ensure my adulthood was better than my childhood, so there was added pressure to follow the straight and narrow.

    Despite my determination, this right or wrong, good or bad, black and white type of thinking to decide *This or That* was quite unpleasant. It caused me to hesitate and become anxious when making decisions. The more I made a "wrong" decision, the lower my confidence became. Nevertheless, my curiosity and critical thinking skills improved. I learned not to accept things at face value. So, I asked questions and checked and double checked; if I found I was on the wrong path, I made a U-turn. Ironically, making a U-turn is much easier on a wide path when you are traveling the broad way. It's never too late to turn around and choose the path less traveled. Sometimes you have to blaze your own trail.

    I include five poems in this section to share instances where I analyzed, questioned, thought critically, and decided between *This or That*.

What is Rain?

Written March 1992

Rain is a sign sent from heaven.
I think it shows joy not pain.
If only I knew what it really meant
that thing the people call rain.

There is more to it than water drops
because it comes from above.
Does it mean laughter, or is it a cry,
or is it showing the world love?

I think it is because people settle down.
They don't hang out in a crowd.
But when the rain stops, people come out.
That's when the town gets loud.

Kids come out and begin to play.
There's loud music everywhere.
But when the rain comes around again
there will be no one there.

When there is no rain around the world,
you hear noise from west to east.
What I think God is trying to do
is show the world peace.

Lyrics

Written May 8, 2005

What a waste of words!
Inner pressures brewing;
like water from a broken spigot,
excrement spewing.

Why are you so enraged
with hate glossed on your lips?
Bruised, leaking heart
drips from your fingertips…

…onto a piece of paper,
but there's no peace,
just degrading lingo,
four-letter words, and sexual fantasies.

What happened to lyrics of love,
tales of everyday life;
when men weren't dogs,
but the husband of one wife?

When chicken heads were cut off,
and we knew that hot things burned.
When women wailed with wisdom,
not with the tongue of the unlearned.

When lonely, begging girls
somehow knew they had a choice.
And even rolling stones
spoke with a repentant voice.

Listen and learn, lyrics are loud,
everlasting, more than a mere phrase.
Be choicy in your choosing; words have weight,
and lips were made for praise.

Plight of a Pusher

Written July 6, 2002

Repetitive, rapid rapping
palpitations start.
False pleasure, no peace
in a loveless heart.
Isolation, fear
out for self; no trust.
Status and power
dominate the lust.
Daily exchanging
green for green,
powder for power,
rocks for cream.
Murder committed,
found guilty.
Sentenced, incarcerated
Second-degree.
Daughters fatherless.
Sons with no guide.
Lack of concern,
blinded by pride.

Fathers, mothers
present yet gone.
Children neglected,
abandoned, alone.
Conscience kicking,
ignored and suppressed.
Focus is survival
no sleep; no rest.
Death occurs
at a pusher's hand.
Murder committed
Second-degree; unplanned.
True transaction,
life for green.
Plight of a Pusher
remains unseen.

Somebody Told You a Lie

Written March 20, 2016

They used to say, "Knowledge is power; education is the key!"
But somebody told you a lie.
They said, "Stay woke; school is for the White man."
So you no longer try.

They used to say, "Reach for the stars, and you'll go far!"
But somebody told you a lie.
Instead of working, these girls be twerking,
Doing just enough to get by.

They used to say "Don't let anyone call you dumb!"
But somebody told you a lie.
The N word means ignorant; it's not a compliment.
Yet, you accept it with no reply.

They used to say, "A mind is a terrible thing to waste!"
But somebody told you a lie.
We'd rather drink and do all types of drugs.
Rather than persevere, we succumb and get high.

They used to say, "Unite and fight for freedom!"
But somebody told you a lie.
To save face and win the rat race,
You believe you must trap or die.

They used to say, "Treat others like you want to be treated!"
But somebody told you a lie.
They say, "Get money and don't snitch!"
Yet, incarceration and murder rates fly.

They used to say "Keep hope alive!"
But somebody told you a lie.
No hope, no pride, we believe the lie.
Inside you slowly die.

Reading Really is Fundamental

Written January 16, 2004

Reading is the foundation of learning.
I grab a book when I get a yearning

To learn new things that I do not know,
And explore places I may never go!

Reading allows me to wander, dream, and imagine.
I can read a comic or even a legend.

It gives me the power to rule as a king.
Through reading, I can do almost anything!

I can read about heroes in biographies,
become a detective through mysteries,

Gain information through various resources,
Meet new characters, hear peculiar voices.

I can read myths, folktales, and fairytales too;
I can read fiction that's fake or nonfiction that's true.

Reading becomes bread when I need a bite to eat;
Grab a book and try it; you'll find it's a treat!

Seven tips to ensure that you'll truly succeed!
READ! READ! READ! READ! READ! READ! READ!

B. Better Than Bitter

After looking for love in all the wrong places, I realized the emotional connection I longed for wasn't going to happen anytime soon. Despite my desires, I knew I had to make a choice.
I could continue to patiently coach whomever I was attempting to date at the time and hope he would adjust and adhere. However, I had tried this approach a few times to no avail. For instance, the guy might pretend he was adhering, and that hurt all the more when I discovered he was not. I would internalize it, thinking there was something wrong with me which added to my distrust and pessimism. I couldn't understand why he wouldn't just do right. If pretending became too much, a few just flat out admitted they would rather fool around, implying that life is too short to settle down.

    I considered playing the game. I started to reevaluate my approach. Was I too serious? After all, I am Type A, and my zodiac sign is Virgo. Was "love" just an illusion of my imagination? Caring wasn't getting me anywhere, so I thought, "If you can't beat them, join them!" Nevertheless, fear kicked in: "What if I get pregnant? What if I catch a disease? Can my heart endure? What about my reputation? Am I capable of not caring? Would I continue to suffer and become bitter?" Who was I kidding? Pretending to not care became burdensome for me as well.

Consequently, I chose to wait. I did not want to settle for less than what I expected. I figured I'd give guys time to grow up, and I chose to stand on what I believed to be right for me. For the majority of my 20s from 2001 to 2008, I did not fully date anyone. I decided I was *Better than Bitter,* so I chose *The Narrow Way.* The six poems in this section reflect the persistent challenge to say, "No, thank you," when the offering is just not good enough.

My Apology

Written May 5, 1995

There's something I want to say to you; it's going to be very hard.
I really want to say it, but I don't know where to start.
I'm going to say it anyway, even after the lies.
The thing I want to say to you is, "I apologize."

I'm sorry for anything I've done to make you feel like me.
I'm sorry for trying to make you be something you didn't want to be.
A man for me, my true love: strong, faithful, and wise.
You'll never be this; now I see. For this, my love, I apologize.

There's something you should say to me. You know it deep down inside.
I know you'll never say it, because of your selfish pride.
All the things you said to me, staring into my eyes.
None of it was true; shouldn't you apologize?

I gave you my love, honesty, and trust. Now I hold all of my feelings inside.
The pain runs deep, the burning is hot. This I'll always hide.
I stood by your side through thick and thin, through the cheating and the lies.
Not once did I see you swallow your pride and say, "My love, I apologize."

There's one thing left for me to say, and then I'll say no more.
I'm sorry I gave my heart away to a boy who walked out the door.
I'm sorry I gave my love, my body, and my pride.
I'm sorry for never going to sleep those nights I stayed up and cried.

Thank you for being strong, staying smart, and being wise.
For this, my soul, I'd like to say, "I apologize!"

Physical

Written September 26, 1995

Fighting the physical leads to defeat
destruction of the soul.
Mental strength is hard to gain
because the physical takes control.

What's good for the physical, is not
always good for the mental,
but physical is always your choice.
Mentally, you are fading away,
so you only hear the physical voice.

Mentally ill they say I am,
but my mind is my only way.
Mental destruction I've received from the world
for physical is the world today.

My mental soars on, for physically I am dust.
Mental is the life I've led.
People of the world are alive physically,
but mentally, they are dead.

Apart

Written February 16, 2002

A part of me longs
And desires you near.
Increasing distance
Brings desperation and fear.

Deeply damaged,
Longing to be complete,
Searching for love,
Attempts lead to defeat.

Calmness subsides
As I peer from afar.
A peaceful presence
Replenishes my scar.

You're there, searching
For purpose, destiny, and will
Disguised with contentment
In reality, unfulfilled.

Epiphany revealed
Clearer than ever.
Separated..........Apart
togrowtogether!

Who?

Written November 8, 2003

Who can be patient, strong, and still
when I say things I regret when I'm keeping it real?

Who can carry the baggage I bring,
my attitude, and my mood that often swings?

When I begin to feel like a motherless child,
who will hold me and relinquish a smile?

Who will love me in spite of me?
Who will be wise and have eyes to see?

The work that is started will one day be complete,
A regenerated being from my head to my feet.

After the process, I'll come out as pure gold
with a renewed heart and mind and a purified soul.

Who will see past the exterior to view the treasure within?
Who can stand the test of time and let their agape love transcend?

Emotions

Written May 24, 2004

Emotions are mere messages from the heart
motivating you to move and magnifying your mood.
One must be manly with amazing manners,
self-motivated to manage and maintain
until the Master's plan is made manifest.
He must manage to be
malleable at the Maker's hand,
while eagerly maximizing each moment.
We shouldn't have to march
for miles and miles to meet a man,
not macho, but mature enough to bring
majesty to the Miracle Worker.
Most men will mask and mistakenly miss
the magnificent and marvelous masterpiece
designed in man's emotions.
The expression of emotions
is the true mark of masculinity.

Contraceptive

Written November 30, 2015

Many have been deceived,
naïve enough to believe,
as long as there's a contraceptive
they can sex whom they please.

No regard for perfection;
preferring an erection over affection,
as long as there's a contraceptive
it negates the need for genuine connection.

Faulty conception breeds disdain
some refrain; others go insane
as long as there's a contraceptive,
why choose to remain?

Making haste when it feels real;
no zeal to seal the deal,
as long as there's a contraceptive,
why forfeit a momentary thrill?

Regret what you accept or
get what you expect
as long as there's a contraceptive
you must cling to self-respect.

Don't be bamboozled
and get got by the game.

There's no contraceptive for . . .

loneliness.

C. *Write the Vision*

They say experience is the best teacher. However, I did not want to become a victim of my circumstances. Despite negative experiences, I saw myself as victorious. Therefore, I knew that at some point I would have to decide who and how I wanted to be if I was truly going to claim the victory. I realized I would have to determine how I wanted to show up and be perceived. What message did I want to send? What mark did I wish to leave?

I found myself periodically composing the counternarratives to refute the negative outcomes that were predicted to be inevitable due to my challenging circumstances. I chose to *Write the Vision* and make it plain, so that I could continue to run and not faint (Habakkuk 2:2; Isaiah 40:31 NKJV). The four poems in this section reflect my written commitment, contracts with myself, outlining what I would eventually become. I revisit these periodically to evaluate where I am, how far I've come, and milestones I have yet to cross.

      The final poem in the section, titled "Through God's Eyes", was the most difficult to compose. I started the poem three years after I completed undergraduate college. I was in my third year of teaching seventh grade at the local middle school in my hometown. After college I moved back home to live with my brother, so I was making efforts to find my way on my own. I knew I couldn't stay with him forever, so I began searching for a condo to purchase in a neighboring town. Fear caused my faith and confidence to fluctuate. I knew what I wanted, but I didn't feel I had acquired the skills and knowledge to fully embrace womanhood even though I had carried the responsibilities of a woman for as long as I could remember. Due to the uncertainty, I pondered the content over the course of a year and seven months before I finally completed the poem.

If

Written June 21, 1995

If I can ease one's heart from breaking,
it shall not be in vain.
If I can bring one smile today,
a friend my soul will gain.

If the thought of me fills your heart with joy,
happiness will fill my soul.
To have my niceness noticed,
unbroken, my heart will be whole.

If I can say a speech that makes you think,
and afterwards, the world is one.
I'll bow my head and lift it with a smile,
And humbly say, "My job is done."

I'll be Leaving Soon

Written September 27, 1996

I'm going somewhere; the time is coming,
for I see I'm in your way.
My journey will end; my voyage will be done,
for I'll be leaving someday.
To you worldly ones, I can't relate.
Why do you choose this life?
You're having fun now, but in the end,
you'll only find grief and strife.

Every time I rise, you knock me down,
but I continue to hold my head up high.
You smack my cheek, but my cheek just turns.
My only remark is, "Why?"
My life has mountains as high as the sky,
deep seas, and oceans blue.
Unlike the valleys and bridges you've crossed,
I've had it much harder than you.

I asked you to come with me,
but to my request, you give no reply.
I leave it at that and continue on.
It's never hurt anyone to try.
Alienated and alone is the way I feel,
but I'll still whistle my tune.
I'm worry free, a change is gonna come,
for I'll be leaving soon.

Abandoned Ship

July 3, 2003

Abandoned Ship
With sails beaten and torn
Decks and mast are weathered
No shine or glisten aboard

Misplaced oars deter the voyage
Drifting to and fro
Waves rhythmically push then pull
Seeming to never let go

Deserted
Left with a loud silence
Seldom creaking
But with hesitance

Because no one hears
Blinded by what appears
To be the damaged exterior
Of what use to be

On a path to a place
Yet drifted off course
Somehow North became South
And South became North

No one to steer
So it floats astray
Stormy winds increase
The guilt and dismay

Oh eyes please see
The abandoned ship
That can be restored
Formed and equipped

For every ship has a treasure
That lies inside
Buried beneath
Hurt shame and pride

There are jewels with great value
Far above a ruby's cost
Still possessing radiant shine
Untainted yet lost

Who will hear the abandoned ship
Pushing against the pressure of the tide
Who will travel the dark corridors
To discover the beauty inside

Who will steer the abandoned ship
Who's drifted so far off course
Who will interpret the creaks and moans
Of a screaming silent voice

Who will teach this ship to sail the sea
Come wind storm or rain
Who will expose and reveal
The treasure behind the pain

Through God's Eyes

Started October 24, 2003- Finished May 10, 2005

Through God's eyes
I'm transparent, clear,
He peers past my doubts,
overlooks my fears.

He doesn't see the wounds
or scars that remain.
Through His eyes they are healed.
He removed the pain.

He doesn't acknowledge
the weakness of my arms
as I shudder at His voice
with disarray and alarm.

He takes no notice
that my feet are lame
as I hesitantly drift
encamped by shame.

He orders my steps,
directs my path,
blots out my sins, and
suppresses His wrath.

My filthy rags
appear as white as snow.
He's the Most High God,
yet sees so low.

My downcast gaze
brings Him no surprise.
Lord, help me to see me
through God's eyes.

Part III:
Free Indeed

Jesus declared, "Come to Me, all you who labor and are heavy laden, and I will give you rest. Take My yoke upon you and learn from Me, for I am gentle and lowly in heart, and you will find rest for your souls. For My yoke is easy and My burden is light." (Matthew 11:28-30 NKJV). Throughout the Bible, there are stories about individuals who pushed through large crowds to reach Jesus, seeking healing from a malady or deliverance from some burdensome circumstance. Time and time again scripture presents Him as a miracle worker, healing the lepers and those who were lame and blind. He also controlled evil through exorcisms and defied nature by walking on water, turning water into wine, and multiplying fish and loaves. He even resurrected the dead in times when it seemed all hope was lost.

I knew that if I was going to live up to my fullest potential, I needed to be free from all fear and self-doubt. Instead of dwelling on the skills and attributes I felt I did not develop due to the lack of mothering, I had to learn to focus on the positive aspects of my life and way of being. I recall around age 20 or 21 reflecting on the lessons I had learned in Sunday school as a child and determining that I needed Jesus to heal my heart. I knew that God had not given me a spirit of fear, but of power and of love and of a sound mind (2 Timothy 1:7 NKJV). Therefore, there was no time for blaming others and continuing in anger. Although I felt weak, I knew He was strong (2 Corinthians 12:9 NKJV). I wanted to be made whole (John 5:6), and I knew that if I allowed the Son to make me free, I would be *Free Indeed* (John 8:36 NKJV). Healing has been an ongoing process, requiring me to cast down all thoughts that try to counter the knowledge of God (2 Corinthians 10:5 NKJV).

The 16 poems in *Part III: Free Indeed* show my quest for confidence and my high hopes for wholeness once I decided I wanted to walk in the fullness of joy (Psalm 16:11 NKJV). Part III is organized in three sections:

A.	Yet Will
B.	Far Above Rubies
C.	Survive to Thrive

A. Yet Will

In the land of Uz beyond the Euphrates River, there once lived a man named Job who was blameless and upright; he feared God and shunned evil (Job 1:1 NKJV). He was blessed with 11 children and an abundance of possessions. He was considered the greatest of all the people of the East (Job 1: 3 NKJV). Nevertheless, the Lord suggested to Satan that he test Job, attacking everything pertaining to him but insisted he spare Job's life (Job 1: 12 NKJV). From there, the test began. Suddenly, Job lost everything, his children, his property, and his possessions. Satan even attacked his health.

Naturally, Job's wife became overwhelmed. Consumed with anxiety, she said, "Do you still hold fast to your integrity? Curse God and die!" His three friends even questioned his faithfulness, and urged him to repent, for surely he had sinned. As a teen I became inspired by Job's response to their faulty conclusions and advice. To his wife, he replied, "You speak as one of the foolish women speaks. Shall we indeed accept good from God, and shall we not accept adversity? To his friends he courageously proclaimed, "Though He [God] slay me, *Yet Will* I trust in Him, and He also shall be my salvation." (Job 13:15-16 NKJV paraphrased). Eventually, the test subsided, and God restored Job to a place of peace and prestige (Job 42 NKJV).

Job's ability to stand and trust God in the face of disappointment and evil encouraged me to believe and persevere in the face of fear and disappointment. *Yet Will* became my mantra during college, and it is one I live by to this day. I wrote the six poems in this section during my 20s. They reflect my trust in and dependency on God during my young adult years as I embraced womanhood.

God the Father

June 17, 2001

He is the…

Giver of life, waiting with

Outstretched hands to

Deliver us from

Temptations and trials.

He never sleeps nor slumbers.

Every promise, He's guaranteed to

Fulfill; every prayer He will

Answer. He is willing and able

To give us the desires of our

Hearts according to His perfect will.

Everything that we need is in His hands.

Rest and believe, our Father is able.

The Prayer I Pray for You

Written June 24, 2001

Dedicated to the few ministers of the Cross who deliver sound doctrine, not for those with itching ears but, to those for whom Jesus is enough (II Timothy 4:3 NKJV).

Father, I see you. You are more than reality.
Sensing your presence, clearly. You are no longer a mystery.
Blinded in darkness and shame. Your face I could not find.
But a voice crying out, so freely, pierced my ear and said, "You're mine."

Quite hard to receive and believe, as fears and doubts crossed my mind.
"How could you love someone like me, so marred from Your original design?"
I had to see the face from whose lips projected life.
"Who could possibly perceive beauty in bitter ashes of hatred and strife?"

Only the lips of one who has been there can bring forth words of restoration.
When I looked, I saw an inner peace that will exalt across the nations.
Reveal that if those lips had not parted and spoke with belief and truth,
This vessel would have remained broken, blemished, and destitute.

Father, help those lips to see that all is not in vain,
And the words that linger from them have taken away my pain.
When it seems like no one's listening and the Word is not received,
Remind them of the captives who hear no Word to believe.

Let them continue to encourage, when all hope seems gone.
With authority and boldness, give them the strength to carry on.
Bringing forth truth and wisdom; raging like a roaring lion.
Show them that they are the lips of a true voice from Zion.

King Solomon's Temple

Written October 2001

Suggested Reading: 2 Chronicles 3-7

Come and see, be mesmerized
in Jerusalem on Mount Moriah.
Where the Spirit of my Lord dwells;
it's sure to take you higher.

Enter into the Most Holy Place,
where even the nails are made of gold;
go behind the linen veil
to rejoice and be made whole.

See Jachin and Boaz,
two pillars standing tall,
reminding that He will establish our strength
if we submit to Him our all.

Witness for yourself the bronzed altar;
kneel and bless His Holy Name,
and like the Queen of Sheba,
your spirit will not remain.

Captivated by its beauty,
gazing as if in a daze,
sounds from the priestly trumpets
will force you to give Him praise.

Bow down and worship;
you're guaranteed to be undone;
when witnessing the temple
built by King Solomon!

Pathway to an Upgrade

Written May 23, 2003

Disgruntled with complacency,
frustrated from lack of progress,
indecisiveness leads to procrastination,
unclear destiny breeds distress.

Heart filled with hesitation,
knees begin to bow,
eyes lifted towards heaven,
seeking an answer now.

"God, I need to hear from you.
I desire to do what's right,
but the path seems so obscure.
I need your lamp as a guiding light."

"I've long awaited your arrival," He replied.
"You see your path has already been laid.
Though the way seems dark, seek My face;
you're on the Pathway to an Upgrade!"

Process for Progress

Written October 13, 2004

Pride and pity
produce pressure
when pursuing God's promise
on the path to
prosperity and productivity.
However, perseverance is possible
if you perceive the prize.
Nevertheless, find
pleasure in pain, and then,
persistence will prevail!

You've Been Drafted

Written January 29, 2007

I got the letter in the mail;
I can't believe I've been selected!
It said report for duty.
Man, the pressure's hectic!

No time to say goodbye
or kiss my family and friends.
Simply put on the whole armor, and
let the games begin!

It said, "To battle, you'll need a sword,
not a semiautomatic.
For the battle's not against flesh and blood
but principalities with strategic war tactics."

"The enemy came to steal,
to kill, and to destroy,
but I offer a life
full of abundance and joy

in the land of the free,
home of the brave,
yet he keeps my people
bound and enslaved."

"But, I'm not prepared!"
was my attempt to avoid,
but there was no escaping the call
for this battle is the Lord's!

"The enemy was slain;
the fight is fixed you see,
but I need your hands
to make the prophecy a reality.

So don't try to fight it;
don't try to flee.
You were chosen before the foundations
to set the captives free!"

B. Far Above Rubies

In the Bible, Proverbs 31 outlines a detailed description of a virtuous wife. I was never one to grieve over not being someone's wife. I decided in my 20s to make the most of life whether married or not. I knew I needed time to evolve and mature, and I was okay with doing that independently and alone. Quite frankly, I had overcome a lot of stressful times early on, so I was not very open to the additional undo stress and drama that dating relationships can sometimes bring. Instead of looking for love, I looked to love myself. I knew my worth was *Far Above Rubies* (Proverbs 31:10 NKJV), and I had no intentions of settling. In the meantime, I worked on becoming virtuous. I devoted my time to my career as an educator, my educational advancement and knowledge, community service, and most importantly, my relationship with Jesus Christ, allowing Him to save me time and time again.

Nevertheless, I still wanted to be loved and appreciated. I also longed for emotional and financial support during hard times when I had to make tough decisions. Furthermore, I craved affirmation. I wanted someone to acknowledge my efforts and declare them satisfactory. But not just someone or anyone, I wanted the right one. I wrote the five poems in this section in my late 20s and early 30s to express my desire to love and be loved and to declare my determination to not settle for less than what I offered.

And let us not grow weary while doing good,
for in due season we shall reap if we do not lose heart.
(Galatians 6:9 NKJV)

Unfulfilled

Written April 29, 2010
...by me for me.

When needs exceed another's desire to remain,
unfulfilled fantasies persist.
Heaviness like snow heaps;
initially, a consuming cold.

Painful,
yet gradually dissipating,
allowing blossoms to bloom amidst emptiness.

The sun will shine again!

Thank You

Written September 22, 2006

Thank you for lending a listening ear,
in no ways deaf, but an ear that can hear.
Thanks for having eyes that can see,
discerning the miracle behind my misery.
Thanks for having lips to speak words of life,
illuminating peace despite the sense of strife.
Thanks for being mature, wise, and true.
Thank you for simply being you!

Falling

Written August 19, 2007

How can falling be so uplifting?
At times I feel I am drifting,
As my mind is constantly shifting
its attention towards you!

    How can falling make me smile,
    Take a drive despite the miles?
    Realizing it's all worthwhile
    For one simple touch from you!

        How can falling be so dear,
        Make me press just to hear
        One soft whisper in my ear,
        Longing to listen to you?

            How can falling make me flutter,
            Cause my lips to release a stutter?
            A fish out of water, I sputter
            From just one glimpse of you!

                How can falling make me dazed,
                As my mind fills with haze?
                Never ceasing to be amazed
                By the kind acts from you!

Normalcy

Written December 26, 2009

A constant craving, for this I seek,
one simple taste of normalcy.

Will desires ever be reality?
Will true love yet find me?

Will family sit at my table to dine?
Will peace ever consume my mind?

Will arms soothe my weary soul?
Will I ever be made whole?

Will my head ever rest upon a lap?
Will I view catastrophes as mere mishaps?

Will thoughts cease to produce tears?
Will God restore the years?

Will my sulk become a smile?
Will I endure the green mile?

Will I resist fleeing the fight?
Will the darkness transition to light?

Will I find a safe place to be weak?
Will I embody mild and meek?

A constant craving, for this I seek,
I must have a taste of normalcy.

Desire

Started May 19, 2004 - Finished June 3, 2010

A man, strong and stable
To protect, you are able
Your acceptance erases rejection
Your eyes reflect affection

Inner beauty, breathtaking
Always real; never faking
Your words, a healing ointment
Orchestrating a divine appointment

Wisdom beyond your years
Yet compassionate, eliminating fears
Heart pleasingly pure
Intrinsic strength to endure

Obstacles, you diminish
Persevering to the finish
Speaking words, right, and true
Confident to press through

Everlasting, never dying
Consistently trying
Never fail, only succeed
Describes the man I want and need

C. Survive to Thrive

When a fellow Christian musters up the courage to tiptoe to the front of the church to give his or her life to Christ during altar call, news spreads. Some whisper it while others shout it, "Such and such (fill in name) got saved today!" Yet, there is a classic, but simple, choir song that I absolutely love by Marvin Winans and Perfected Praise. It's called "Jesus Saves", and the lyrics say, "To the utmost, Jesus saves! To the utmost, Jesus saves! He will pick you up and turn you around, Hallelujah, hallelujah, hallelujah, Jesus saves!" As a lover of language, I pay attention to word choice and tense, and one day the lyrics to that song clicked for me...Jesus SAVES! It dawned on me that salvation is continuous, not a one-time event.

The Lord is my strength and my song, and He has become my salvation (Psalm 118:14 NKJV). He is the Way, the Truth, and the Life (John 14:6 NKJV). When I feel as if I am overwhelmed by the trials of life, He never fails to rescue and restore me to a place of wholeness and hope. He is (present tense) my salvation, even now. Therefore, in turbulent times, I am reminded, I shall not die, but live, and declare the works of the Lord (Psalm 118:17 NKJV). Jesus proclaimed, "I have come that they may have life and that they may have it more abundantly" (John 10:10 NKJV). Therefore, I believe we were born to not simply *Survive* but to *Thrive!*

I have come to know that we evolve, and life's lessons are unending. Therefore, be patient with yourself and ever-learning. When it seems you can't take anymore, give! Besides, the world already has enough takers. The five poems in this section highlight my persistence and resilience to realize my full potential. I encourage you to persevere; we need you! Repeat after me:

Despite the ebbs and flows of life,
I refuse to be stressed.
Of all the things to be,
I choose bold, beautiful, and blessed!

Make It Happen

March 18, 2001

Motivate yourself

Acknowledge your need for God

Keep the faith

Exercise your gifts

Invest in your future

Touch and agree

Halt all complaining

Ask and ye shall receive

Plan, prepare, and pray

Press toward the goal

Encourage your fellow man

Never give up

Manners Matter

Written April 2005

Always
Be
Caring
Doing
Extraordinary
Favors,
Giving,
Helping
Intensely.
Just
Know
Love
Moves
Nastiness
Over.
Politeness
Quickens
Righteousness.
Sincerity
Teaches
Unusual
Victory
With
X-treme
Youthful
Zeal.

Bold and Beautiful Brooksie

Written April 2005

Being the best I can be to

Reach the raised rooftop. I'm

Outrageously outgoing and

Oftentimes optimistic.

Kindness kills, so I am

Sensitive, suave, and sometimes silly.

I invest in intellect because

Excellence and esteem exceed everything!

Questions, Comments, or Concerns?

Written September 3, 2013 - Finished May 10, 2015

This is why I grind.
This is why I choose to be fine.

This is why I laugh vs. cry.
This is how I get better, not just get by.

This is why I give vs. take.
This is why I acknowledge my mistakes.

This is how I maintain hope.
This is how I refrain from dope.

This is why I run vs. walk.
This is why I listen vs. balk.

This is why I speak vs. cease.
This is how I preserve my peace.

This is how I overcome death.
I grasp the moments that give me breath.

Fly, Fly Away

Written July 24, 2010

Caterpillars hide
Cocoons conceal
Stagnant
Sluggish
Time will reveal

Oh, but a butterfly
Beautiful
Spry
Flee your cocoon
Those wings were made to fly!

About the Author

Dr. Brooksie Broome Sturdivant is an educational leader, award-winning researcher, author, and poet. Having served in public education as a teacher, literacy coach, curriculum facilitator, equity specialist, and professor, Dr. Sturdivant is most passionate about student empowerment. She speaks with provocative passion influenced by her experience with household dysfunction and childhood neglect.

She is a native of Walnut Cove, NC, a rural town in Stokes County. She currently resides in Raleigh, NC with her husband, Norlonn A. Sturdivant. Dr. Sturdivant believes we can truly achieve Equity and Empowerment through Education, which she promotes through her company, 3e LLC.

For additional information, visit www.3ellc.org.

Made in the USA
Columbia, SC
24 January 2023